MEET THE PRESIDENTS

A Book To Color

by Nancy E. Krulik

Pictures by Robert Roper

SCHOLASTIC INC.
New York   Toronto   London   Auckland   Sydney

No part of this publication may be reproduced
in whole or in part, or stored in a retrieval
system, or transmitted in any form or by any
means, electronic, mechanical, photocopying,
recording, or otherwise, without written
permission of the publisher. For information
regarding permission, write to Scholastic Inc.,
730 Broadway, New York, NY 10003.

ISBN 0-590-41977-3

Copyright © 1988 by Scholastic Books, Inc. All rights reserved. Published by Scholastic Inc.

12 10 9 8 7 6 5 4   2 3/9

Printed in the U.S.A.   34

First Scholastic printing, September 1988

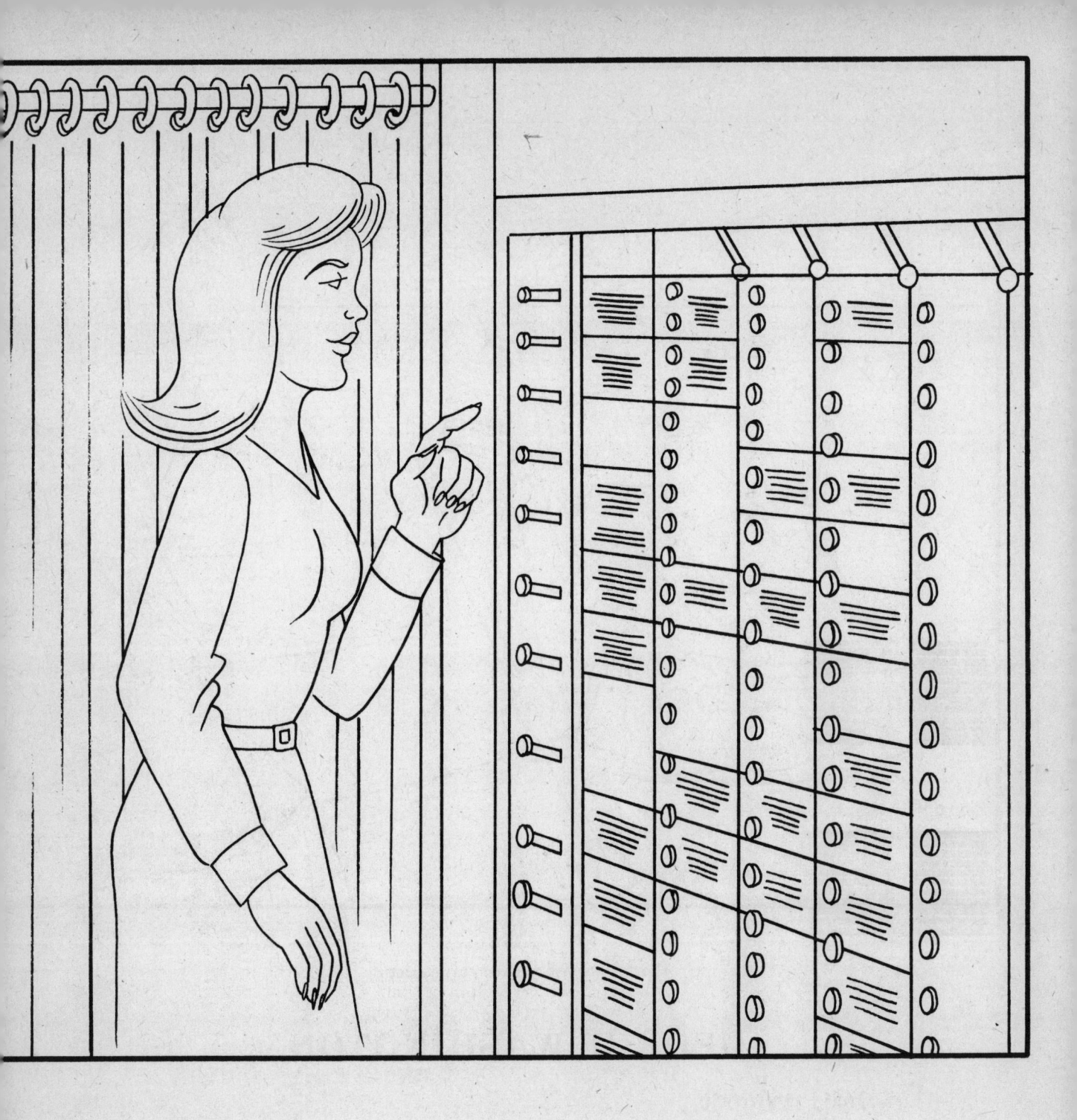

Every four years, Americans elect a new President. Election Day is the first Tuesday after the first Monday in November.

GEORGE WASHINGTON

1st President

Born: February 22, 1732   *Died:* December 14, 1799
Term of Office: 1789–1797

Before he was elected President, George Washington was the leader of the Colonial Army during the Revolutionary War.
In one famous fight, he led the troops across the Delaware River.

JOHN ADAMS

2nd President

Born: October 30, 1735   *Died:* July 4, 1826
Term of Office: 1797–1801

John Adams was America's first Vice-President. Later, he was the first President to live in the White House.

THOMAS JEFFERSON

3rd President

Born: April 13, 1743 *Died:* July 4, 1826
Term of Office: 1801–1809

Thomas Jefferson wrote the Declaration of Independence in 1776.

JAMES MADISON

4th President

Born: March 16, 1751 *Died:* June 28, 1836
Term of Office: 1809–1817

While James Madison was in the White House,
British soldiers set it on fire.
President Madison and his wife Dolley ran for safety.
Dolley remembered to take all of her jewels and furs.

JAMES MONROE

5th President

Born: April 28, 1758   *Died:* July 4, 1831
Term of Office: 1817–1825

James Monroe was the first President to ride on a steamboat.
The boat was called the *Savannah*.

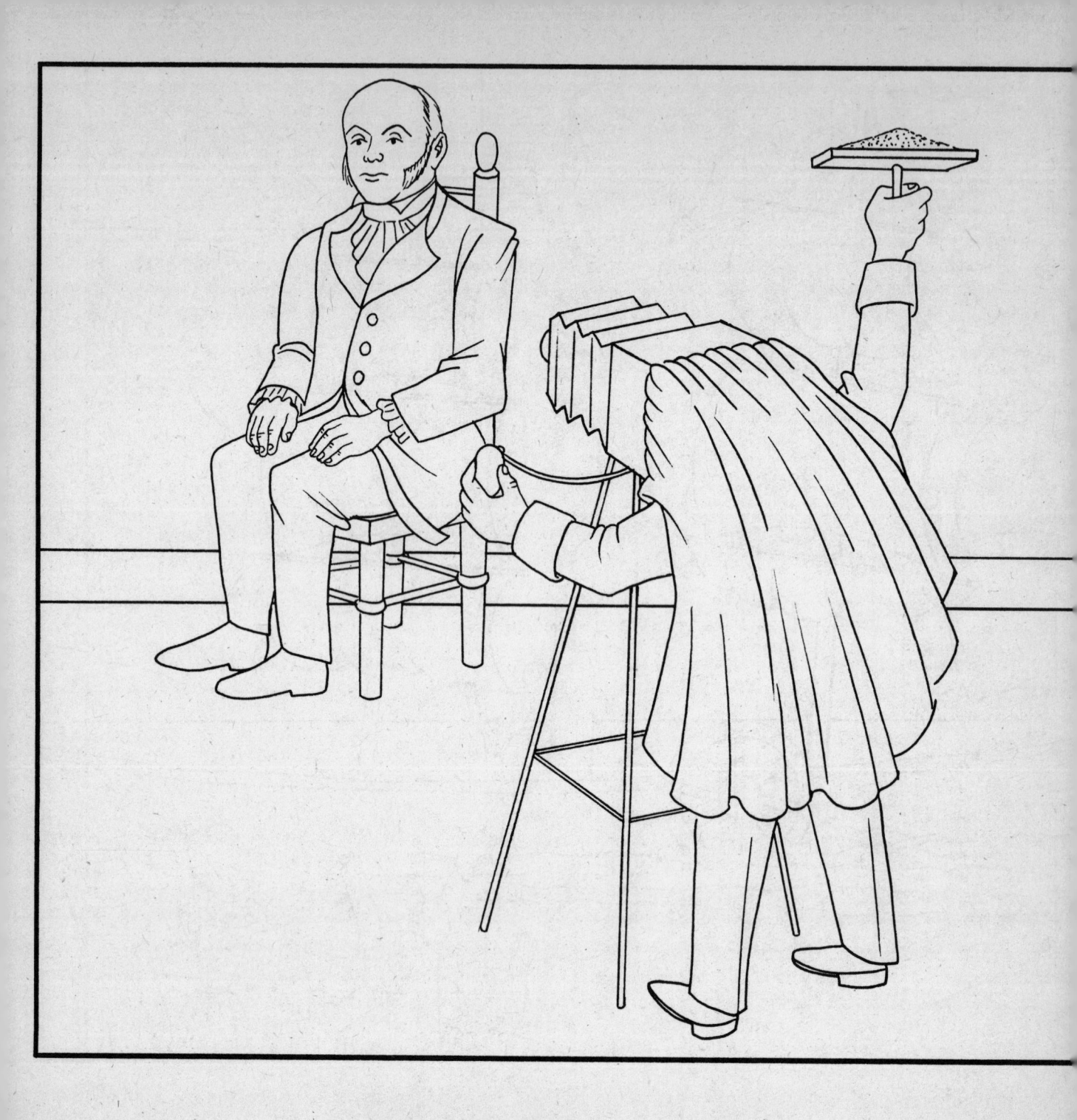

JOHN QUINCY ADAMS

6th President

Born: July 11, 1767 *Died:* February 23, 1848
Term of Office: 1825–1829

John Quincy Adams was the son of
President John Adams.
He was also the first President
to have his picture taken.

ANDREW JACKSON

7th President

Born: March 15, 1767 *Died:* June 8, 1845
Term of Office: 1829–1837

Andrew Jackson was the first President born
in a log cabin.
He loved animals so much, he had a stable of horses
at the White House.

MARTIN VAN BUREN

8th President

Born: December 5, 1782 *Died:* July 24, 1862
Term of Office: 1837–1841

Martin Van Buren was a very small man.
His friends called him "Little Van."
Before he became President,
Martin Van Buren was a lawyer.
Sometimes he had to stand on a table to talk to the jury.

WILLIAM HENRY HARRISON

9th President

Born: February 9, 1773 *Died:* April 4, 1841
Term of Office: March 4, 1841–April 4, 1841

William Henry Harrison became President
on a cold and rainy day.
But he decided to ride a horse in a parade in his
honor anyway.
President Harrison got very sick from this
and died one month later.

JOHN TYLER

10th President

Born: March 29, 1790 *Died:* January 18, 1862
Term of Office: 1841–1845

John Tyler had 15 children.
He was playing marbles with some of his children when he found out he had become President.

JAMES KNOX POLK

11th President

Born: November 2, 1795 *Died:* June 15, 1849
Term of Office: 1845–1849

James Knox Polk was the first President to have a speech sent out to newspapers over a telegraph machine.
Samuel Morse, the man who invented the telegraph, tapped the speech onto the machine.

ZACHARY TAYLOR

12th President

Born: November 24, 1784   *Died:* July 9, 1850
Term of Office: 1849–1850

Zachary Taylor was a soldier.
He rode a horse named Whitey when he fought.
Later, President Taylor brought Whitey to the White House to live.
Whitey ate the grass on the White House lawn.

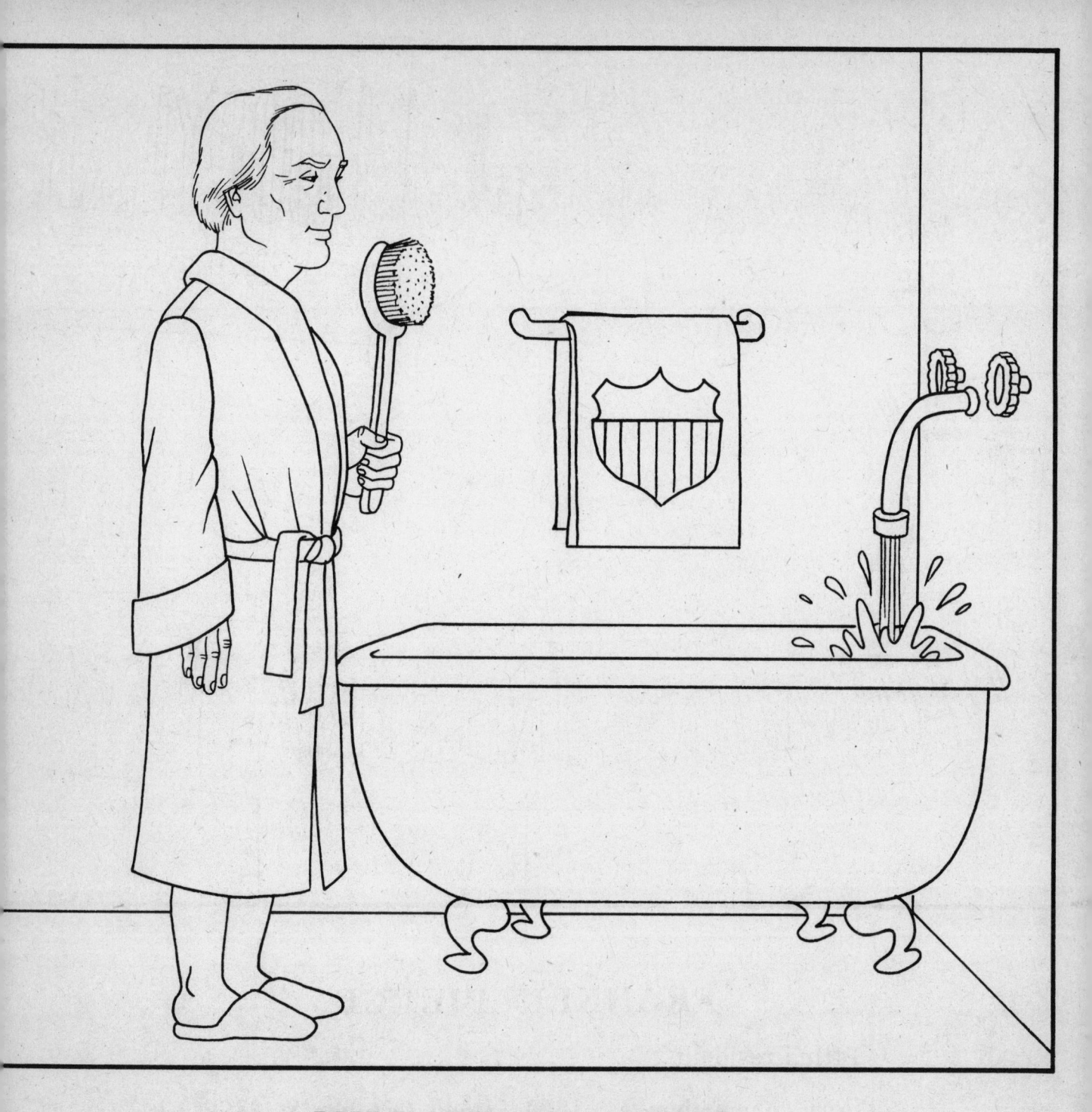

MILLARD FILLMORE

13th President

Born: January 7, 1800 *Died:* March 8, 1874
Term of Office: 1850–1853

Millard Fillmore worked hard to make the White House more modern.
He had a cast-iron stove put in for cooking, and plumbers installed the first White House bathtub with running water.

FRANKLIN PIERCE

14th President

Born: November 23, 1804   *Died:* October 8, 1869
Term of Office: 1853–1857

When Franklin Pierce was President,
all sorts of machines were being invented.
In 1853, he was the first guest at a special fair
where many of the machines were shown.

JAMES BUCHANAN

15th President

Born: April 23, 1791 *Died:* June 1, 1868
Term of Office: 1857–1861

James Buchanan was the only President
who was never married.
On August 16, 1858, he sent the first
telegraph message across the Atlantic Ocean.
The message was to England's Queen Victoria.

When he was young, Abraham Lincoln was too poor to buy books. He walked many miles to borrow them from neighbors.

In 1862, President Lincoln told most of the slave owners to free their slaves.

ABRAHAM LINCOLN

16th President

Born: February 12, 1809 *Died:* April 15, 1865
Term of Office: 1861–1865

Even when he was President, Abraham Lincoln always took time to read to his son Tad.

President Lincoln visited many army camps during the Civil War.

ANDREW JOHNSON

17th President

Born: December 29, 1808 *Died:* July 31, 1875
Term of Office: 1865–1869

Andrew Johson never went to school. He taught himself to read and write while he learned to be a tailor.

ULYSSES SIMPSON GRANT

18th President

Born: April 27, 1822 *Died:* July 23, 1885
Term of Office: 1869–1877

Ulysses S. Grant was in charge of all the Northern troops in the Civil War.
In 1865, he won the war when
General Robert E. Lee, leader of the Southern troops, surrendered in a town called Appomattox, Virginia.

RUTHERFORD BIRCHARD HAYES

19th President

Born: October 4, 1822 *Died:* January 17, 1893
Term of Office: 1877–1881

Rutherford B. Hayes was the first President
to talk on a telephone in the White House.
Alexander Graham Bell,
the man who invented the telephone,
showed President Hayes how to use it.

JAMES ABRAM GARFIELD

20th President

Born: November 19, 1831 *Died:* September 19, 1881
Term of Office: March 4, 1881–September 19, 1881

James A. Garfield could speak many languages.
He liked to amaze people by writing in Greek
with one hand, and writing in Latin
with the other hand — at the same time!

CHESTER ALAN ARTHUR

21st President

Born: October 5, 1829 *Died:* November 18, 1886
Term of Office: 1881–1885

Chester A. Arthur thought the White House
was gloomy.
When he became President,
he bought new furniture for his new home.
It took 24 wagons to cart away
the old White House furniture.

GROVER CLEVELAND

22nd and 24th President

Born: March 18, 1837   *Died:* June 24, 1908
Terms of Office: 1885–1889 (first term)
                   1893–1897 (second term)

Grover Cleveland was the only President to get married in the White House. He is also the only man to be President for four years, and then become President again four years later.

BENJAMIN HARRISON

23rd President

Born: August 20, 1833 *Died:* March 13, 1901
Term of Office: 1889–1893

Benjamin Harrison was the grandson of President William Henry Harrison. He was the last President to wear a beard, and the first one to sign papers by an electric light.

WILLIAM McKINLEY

25th President

Born: January 29, 1843   *Died:* September 14, 1901
Term of Office: 1897–1901

William McKinley was the last President
to have fought in the Civil War.
When he was a soldier, he drove a coffee wagon
onto the battlefields.
He served other soldiers coffee.

THEODORE ROOSEVELT

26th President

Born: October 27, 1858 *Died:* January 6, 1919
Term of Office: 1901–1909

Before he was President,
Theodore Roosevelt was a famous jungle explorer.
The teddy bear is named for
President Theodore "Teddy" Roosevelt.

WILLIAM HOWARD TAFT

27th President

Born: September 15, 1857 *Died:* March 8, 1930
Term of Office: 1909–1913

William Howard Taft was the first President
to toss out the first ball
at the start of the baseball season.
He threw out the ball that opened the 1910
baseball season.

WOODROW WILSON

28th President

Born: December 28, 1856 *Died:* February 3, 1924
Term of Office: 1913–1921

Women earned the right to vote while Woodrow Wilson was President.

WARREN GAMALIEL HARDING

29th President

Born: November 2, 1865 *Died:* August 2, 1923
Term of Office: 1921–1923

When he was 19 years old,
Warren G. Harding and two friends
bought a newspaper, *The Marion* (Ohio) *Star*.
The paper became a big success.

CALVIN COOLIDGE

30th President

Born: July 4, 1872 *Died:* January 5, 1933
Term of Office: 1923–1929

Calvin Coolidge loved animals.
One of his pets was a raccoon named Rebecca.
He walked her on a leash.

HERBERT CLARK HOOVER

31st President

Born: August 10, 1874 *Died:* October 20, 1964
Term of Office: 1929–1933

Before he became President,
Herbert Hoover was a scientist.
He studied rocks and metals.
He and his wife Lou found gold in Australia
and China.

FRANKLIN DELANO ROOSEVELT

32nd President

Born: January 30, 1882 *Died:* April 12, 1945
Term of Office: 1933–1945

Franklin Roosevelt talked to America over the radio.
He called these talks "Fireside Chats."
President Roosevelt had to sit in a wheelchair.
After having polio, he could not use his legs.
He was President for 12 years.
That's longer than any other President.

HARRY S TRUMAN

33rd President

Born: May 8, 1884   *Died:* December 26, 1972
Term of Office: 1945–1953

Harry S Truman was the first President to give a speech on television.

DWIGHT DAVID EISENHOWER

34th President

Born: October 14, 1890   *Died:* March 28, 1969
Term of Office: 1953–1961

Before he became President,
Dwight D. Eisenhower was a general in the Army.
He was also the only President to have a pilot's
license.

JOHN FITZGERALD KENNEDY

35th President

Born: May 29, 1917   *Died:* November 22, 1963
Term of Office: 1961–1963

John F. Kennedy was a skipper in the Navy.
He was in charge of a boat called *PT 109*.
When the boat was destroyed in a sea battle,
John Kennedy helped save many men's lives.
He was given a medal for bravery.

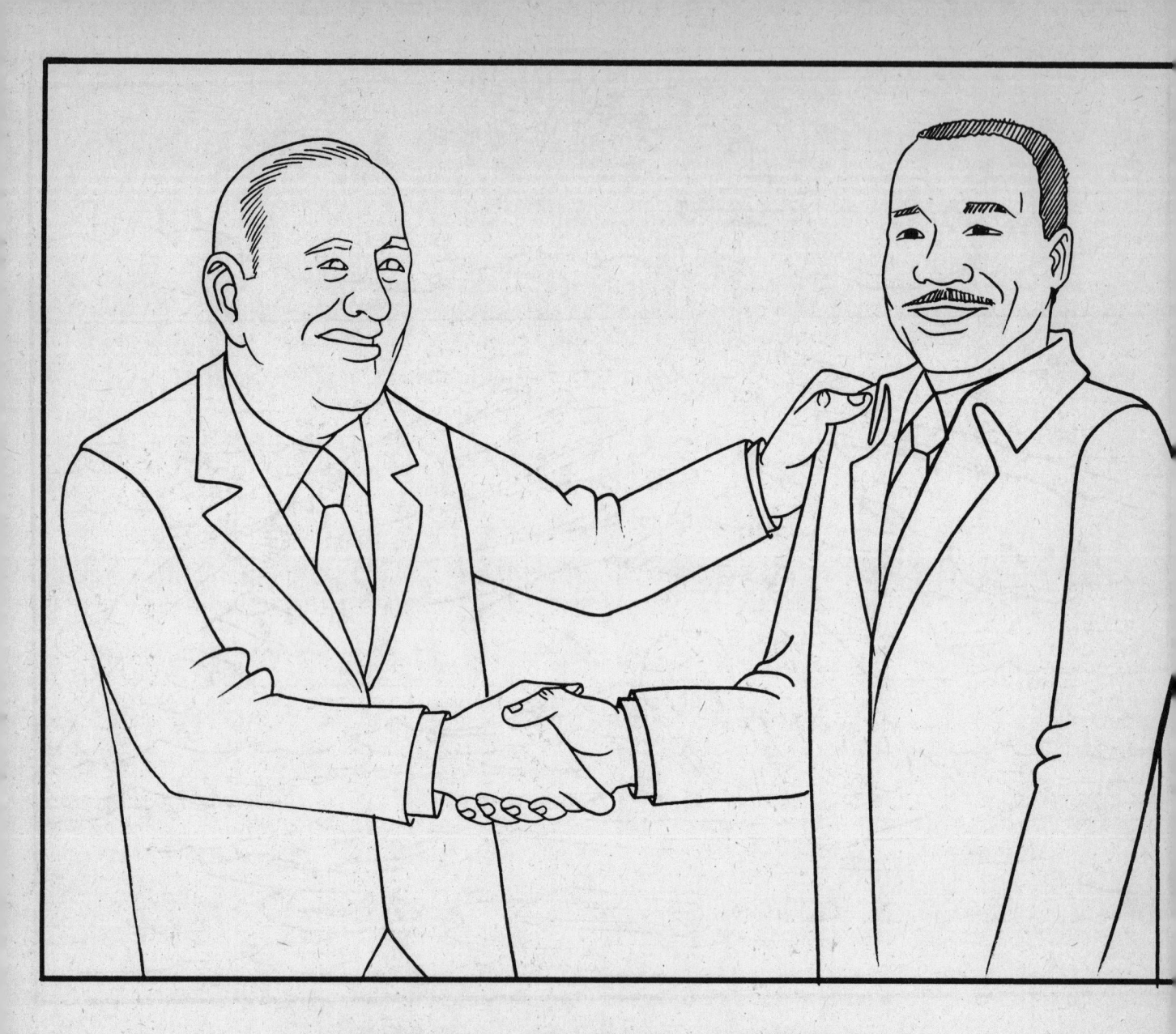

LYNDON BAINES JOHNSON

36th President

Born: August 27, 1908 *Died:* January 22, 1973
Term of Office: 1963–1969

President Johnson signed a law
that gave black people many rights
they did not have before.
This made many black leaders,
like Dr. Martin Luther King, Jr., very happy.

RICHARD MILHOUS NIXON

37th President

Born: January 9, 1913
Term of Office: 1969–1974

Richard Nixon was the first President to visit China.
He was also the first President to talk to a man on the moon.

GERALD RUDOLPH FORD

38th President

Born: July 14, 1913
Term of Office: 1974–1977

Gerald Ford was an all-star football player in college.
President Ford was the only President
not elected by the American people.
President Nixon made him Vice-President.
He became President
when President Nixon left office.

JAMES EARL CARTER

39th President

Born: October 1, 1924
Term of Office: 1977–1981

Jimmy Carter grew up on his family's peanut farm.
He became governor of Georgia,
and then he became President.
While he was President, he helped Israel
and Egypt sign their first peace treaty.

RONALD REAGAN

40th President

Born: February 6, 1911
Term of Office: 1981–1989

In 1987 President Reagan signed a treaty with Mikhail Gorbachev, the leader of the Soviet Union. The treaty helped get rid of some nuclear weapons.

Name: _____

41st President

Born: _____
Term of Office: 1989–

Who will be the next President?
Fill in the blanks.
Draw a picture of the new President.

The new President is sworn in on January 20.
The new President promises to try to be a good President.

If you would like to write a letter to the President, this is the address:

The President of the United States
The White House
1600 Pennsylvania Avenue
Washington, DC 20500

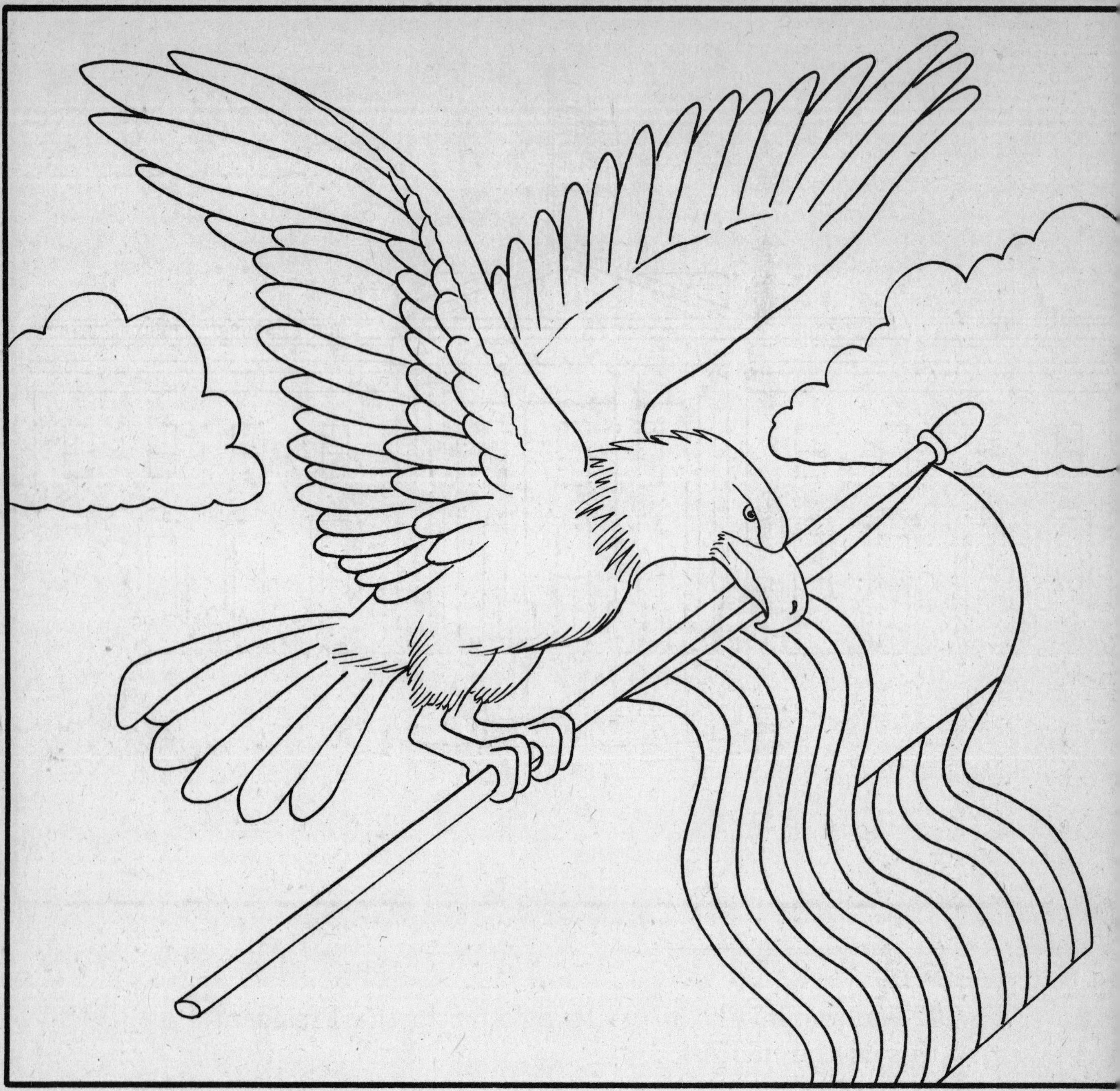